D1409801

9/04

j 629.2275 Tiner

Tiner, J.
Motorcycles.
Kitchener Public Library
Forest Heights-Childrens
Non-fiction

Published by Creative Education
123 South Broad Street, Mankato, Minnesota 56001
Creative Education is an imprint of The Creative Company

Art direction by Rita Marshall
Production design by The Design Lab

Photographs by Corbis (Sheldan Collins, Patrick Ward), Hulton Archive, Derk R. Kuyper,
Sally McCrae Kuyper, Craig Lovell, Doug Mitchel, Wernher Krutein (photovault.com),
Underwood Photo Archives, Unicorn Stock Photos (Bachmann)

Copyright © 2004 Creative Education.
International copyrights reserved in all countries.
No part of this book may be reproduced in any form
without written permission from the publisher.
Printed in the United States of America.

Library of Congress Cataloging-in-Publication Data

Tiner, John Hudson, 1944–
Motorcycles / by John Hudson Tiner.
p. cm. — (Let's investigate)
Summary: Provides information on riding a motorcycle, motorcycle
engines, the various uses of motorcycles, and presents a relevant
historical timeline.
ISBN 1-58341-285-9
1. Motorcycles—Juvenile literature. [1. Motorcycles.] I. Title. II. Series.
TL440.15 .T56   2003
629.227'5—dc21   2002034867

First edition

2 4 6 8 9 7 5 3 1

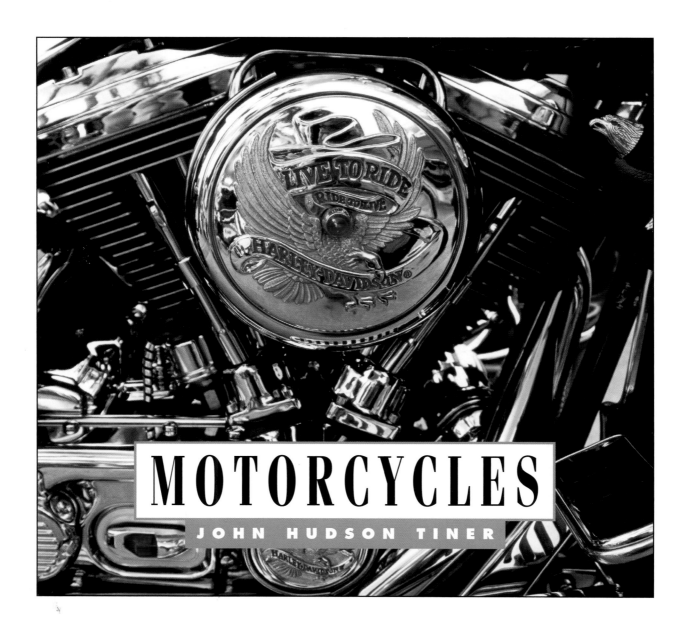

MOTORCYCLES

JOHN HUDSON TINER

Creative Education

MOTORCYCLE
MOVIE

The 1954 movie The Wild One *was about a violent motorcycle gang. The movie and others like it helped give all motorcycle riders a reputation for being unruly.*

Motorcycles appeal to different people for different reasons

Motorcycles are a popular form of transportation around the world. People in poorer countries ride them because small motorcycles are inexpensive to buy, operate, and repair. In Europe, where many cities have narrow, crowded streets, motorcycles are a speedy way to travel. And in the United States, more than six million riders enjoy cruising along the open road on motorcycles.

MOTORCYCLE

Gottlieb Daimler's 1885 motorcycle had a wooden frame and wheels with iron rims. The ride was so uncomfortable that the machine was nicknamed the "bone crusher."

6

MOTORCYCLE ENGINES

The first motorcycles were built by putting a motor on a bicycle. Gottlieb Daimler, a German inventor, built the first motorcycle with a gasoline engine. Daimler's 17-year-old son Paul became the first motorcycle rider in 1885. His first ride around the town of Cannstatt, Germany, covered a distance of 10 miles (16 km).

Motorcycles originated in Germany and soon spread to other countries

Motorcycles were improved by using smaller but more powerful engines. An engine gets its power by burning gasoline mixed with air inside a chamber called the cylinder. A **spark plug** produces an electric spark that ignites the fuel. The hot, expanding gases push against a piston in the cylinder, causing the piston to pump up and down. The **crankshaft**, gears, and a chain move the power of the piston to the rear wheel and put the motorcycle in motion.

Chains similar to those on a bicycle help to turn a motorcycle's wheels

MOTORCYCLE
P O W E R

Most motorcycles use a metal chain or belt to carry power from the engine to the rear wheel. However, a few motorcycles use a spinning metal rod called a drive shaft.

MOTORCYCLE
C L A S S E S

Motocross racers compete against one another in classes based on the size of the motorcycles' engines—125 cc, 250 cc, or 500 cc.

Generally, the more cylinders an engine has, the faster the cycle can go

Some small engines have only one cylinder. Larger and more powerful engines have two, four, or more cylinders. The size of an engine is described by the amount of space inside the cylinder in cubic centimeters, abbreviated cc. In a small motorcycle with a single cylinder, the total size is about 50 cc (three cubic inches). When the sizes of all the cylinders are added together, the largest motorcycle engines have a size of about 1,500 cc (92 cubic inches).

Small motorcycles have two-stroke engines. A stroke is the movement of the piston up or down inside the cylinder. As the piston moves down, it draws in gasoline and air through an opening called the intake port. At the same time, the burned gasoline fumes are forced out through the exhaust port on the other side. The piston comes back up, compresses the gasoline and air, and fires again. The piston makes two strokes—down and back up—between each time the spark plug fires.

Larger motorcycles have four-stroke engines that generate more power and get better **gas mileage** than two-stroke engines. An average-sized motorcycle with a four-stroke engine can go 50 to 100 miles (80–161 km) on one gallon (3.8 l) of gasoline.

MOTORCYCLE
H E A T

An engine gets hot as it runs. Two-stroke motorcycle engines have metal cooling fins on the outside of the cylinder. Air rushing by the fins carries away excess heat.

9

Skilled mechanics can keep a motorcycle engine of any size in peak condition

MOTORCYCLE

F I R S T

In 1914, the Indian Motorcycle Company built the first motorcycle with an electric starter. The company went out of business in 1953 when Japanese motorcycles became popular.

MOTORCYCLE MAKERS

In the early 1900s, one of the best-known American makers of motorcycles was the Indian Motorcycle Company. In 1901, bicycle racer George Hendee and inventor Oscar Hedstrom built a motorized bicycle in their shop in Springfield, Massachusetts. Their first motorcycle, which they called the Indian, had a top speed of 30 miles (48 km) per hour. They started a company, and by 1914, they were selling about 20,000 Indian motorcycles a year. In 1920, an Indian with a 994-cc engine set a speed record of 104 miles (167 km) per hour. It was the first motorcycle to officially go faster than 100 miles (161 km) per hour.

In 1903, two friends—William Harley and Arthur Davidson—decided to make a motorcycle. They worked in a wooden shed behind Davidson's home in Milwaukee,

This Indian motorcycle, built in 1912, was basically a bicycle with an engine

MOTORCYCLE
M O D E L S

The best-known American-made motorcycle is the Harley-Davidson. This popular brand has models with such names as the Electra Glide, Super Glide, and Low Rider.

MOTORCYCLE
E N G I N E S

Four-stroke engines do a better job of keeping the exhaust gas and fuel from mixing together, so they are less polluting than two-stroke engines.

Wisconsin. Their first motorcycle had a top speed of only 25 miles (40 km) per hour, but they created improved models and began selling them. By 1909, Harley-Davidson motorcycles could travel at a speed of 60 miles (97 km) per hour.

"Harleys" quickly earned a reputation as quality, durable motorcycles

MOTORCYCLE
N A M E

The first Harley-Davidson motorcycles, built for sale in 1904, ran quietly and were painted gray. The dependable machines were called the Silent Gray Fellows.

This Electra Glide from Harley-Davidson has a typical heavy metal build

Like other motorcycles, Harley-Davidson motorcycles had iron frames, steel engines, and metal fenders. A person had to be strong to merely keep them upright. The bikes weighed about 900 pounds (410 kg), and riders sometimes suffered broken bones when motorcycles tipped over on them. Harley-Davidson engines made a loud, rumbling sound, and because of their large size, the motorcycles became known as "hogs."

In the 1950s, Japanese companies began selling motorcycles that were small, lightweight, and inexpensive. Many young motorcycle riders liked the nimble Japanese motorcycles better than the loud and heavy American-made ones. The sudden popularity of Japanese motorcycles made by Honda, Kawasaki, Yamaha, and Suzuki became known as the "Japanese invasion." The Japanese motorcycles did so well that the Indian Motorcycle Company lost its customers and had to go out of business. Harley-Davidson survived, though, and is still making motorcycles for people who like to ride big and powerful machines.

MOTORCYCLE
POPULARITY

Honda motorcycles, first made in 1949, are named after Honda Soichiro, a Japanese engineer. In 1959, Hondas became the best-selling motorcycles in the world, a status they still enjoy.

13

Above, the aggressive styling of a Honda Left, a Suzuki motorcycle from the 1960s

MOTORCYCLE

DECOR

On most motorcycles, the fuel tank is above the engine and between the seat and handlebars. Many riders have artists paint designs on the fuel tank.

MOTORCYCLE

BRAKING

Harley-Davidson motorcycles featured the first front wheel brakes in 1928. Many riders believed brakes in front would cause the motorcycle to flip end over end, but this proved untrue.

A motorcycle is much heavier than a bicycle and involves more controls

RIDING A MOTORCYCLE

Riding a motorcycle is not as simple as riding a bicycle. A motorcycle rider moves controls such as the **throttle**, handlebars, and brakes to change speed, turn, and stop. Today, controls are in a standard position on all motorcycles. Like a bicycle, the handlebars turn the motorcycle. The rider leans into turns to keep the motorcycle from tipping over.

The right handlebar has a grip that the rider rotates to give the engine gas, and a brake lever for the front wheel. The left handlebar has a **clutch** lever for shifting gears. The handlebars also have buttons for turning on lights to signal left or right turns, sounding the horn, and starting the motor. Mirrors are attached to the handlebars so the rider can see what is behind the motorcycle.

MOTORCYCLE
R U L E S

Motorcycles can be driven on city streets only if they have the required equipment— lights, mirrors, horn, muffler, and license. Such bikes are described as being "street legal."

15

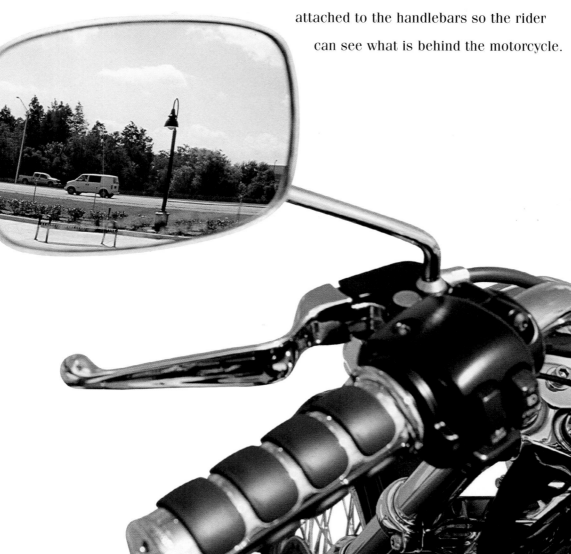

Motorcycle riders rely on rear-view mirrors to see what is behind them

Motorcycle tires made for highway use have grooves (tread) that channel away water when the roads are slick with rain. Tires for use on snow and ice are covered with metal studs and spikes.

he rider's feet are busy, too. The left side of a motorcycle has a foot pedal for shifting gears, and the right side has the brake lever for the rear wheel. Some small motorcycle engines have a kick-starter. After flipping out a small lever attached to the motor, the rider suddenly puts all of his or her weight on the lever. This starts the motor.

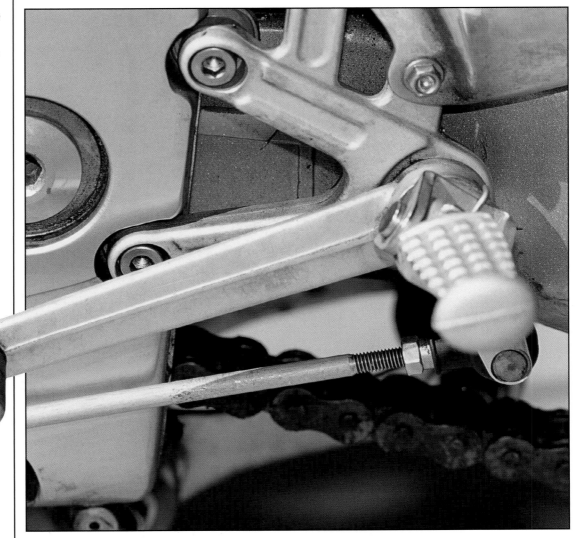

A motorcycle's left foot peg, with the gear shift pedal just in front of it

There are several instruments between a motorcycle's handlebars. A speedometer shows the speed in miles or kilometers per hour. A fuel gauge shows the amount of fuel in the gas tank. And warning lights come on if the engine overheats or is running low on oil.

MOTORCYCLE
CHANGE

A motorcycle that has been customized (changed) by the owner is called a chopper. The first choppers usually had high handlebars and a long fork holding the front wheel.

Left, motorcycle instruments
Below, a chopper

MOTORCYCLE
SAFETY

Regardless of where a motorcycle is used, riders need to be trained, wear safety equipment, and operate the machine carefully and responsibly.

Whether cruising for fun or racing, riders should always wear protective gear

Many motorcycle riders wear crash helmets to protect their head, goggles or visors to shield their eyes, and leather jackets to cover their skin. If a rider wipes out and skids along the roadway, it is much better to wear away a cowhide jacket than human skin. Most states in America, and many countries such as Canada, require all motorcycle riders to wear helmets.

MOTORCYCLES AT WORK

During World War I (1914–1918), motorcycles served as a rapid way to carry messages. Motorcycle scouts rode ahead of advancing armies to check out the condition of roads and the location of the enemy. Some motorcycles were outfitted with **sidecars**. The sidecar carried a soldier who operated a machine gun. During battle, other motorcycles with sidecars carried wounded soldiers to field hospitals. Some armies today have small, rugged motorcycles that can be dropped by parachutes.

MOTORCYCLE
REVERSAL

During World War I (1914–1918), the Indian Motorcycle Company built motorcycles for the U.S. Army with the throttle on the left handlebar so right-handed soldiers could hold their weapons as they rode.

German soldiers riding sidecar-equipped motorcycles during World War II

19

MOTORCYCLE

In 1999, about 2,500 motorcycle riders and passengers died in traffic accidents in the U.S. That was better than in 1975, when 3,300 died on the road.

Police departments appreciate the benefits of motorcycles. Because city streets can be very crowded, some police officers ride motorcycles to quickly reach the scenes of crimes or accidents. Police motorcycles, called cruisers, have powerful, 1,200-cc engines. Some cities, such as London, England, are experimenting with sending **medics** to the scenes of accidents on specially equipped ambulance motorcycles.

Police cruisers can move at high speeds and navigate around traffic jams

Some people ride motorcycles because they are an inexpensive way to get around in a city. The simplest motorcycle is a motorized pedal bicycle, called a moped, which weighs about 130 pounds (60 kg) and has a 50-cc, two-stroke engine. Mopeds and slightly larger motor scooters and minibikes are popular in countries where gasoline is expensive. Their top speed is about 35 miles (56 km) per hour.

MOTORCYCLE
PROTECTION

Off-road motorcycle riders dress to prepare for the dangers of crashes and flying gravel. They wear leather pants, chest protectors, kneepads, armored gloves, and boots with steel toes.

Mopeds and minibikes make a whining noise as they zip around town

MOTORCYCLE

The first motorcycle to go faster than 300 miles (483 km) per hour was the Yamaha Silver Bird, driven in 1975 by Don Vesco at the Bonneville speedway in Utah.

22

MOTORCYCLE
E N D U R A N C E

Enduro *races may cover 5,000 miles (8,050 km) and last a week or more. They are usually run over rough terrain such as the outback of Australia or the deserts of Africa.*

For greater speed and longer trips on highways, motorcyclists ride touring bikes. These big motorcycles have comfortable seats and compartments over the rear wheel to carry clothing or other gear. A touring motorcycle may have a seat for a second rider behind the main seat. The driver and rider can talk to one another through an intercom system that plugs into their helmets. When fully loaded with equipment and riders, a touring motorcycle may weigh up to 1,200 pounds (544 kg)—about half as much as a car.

MOTORCYCLE
DISTANCE

The Paris-Dakar race covers 9,000 miles (14,500 km) from Paris, France, through the Sahara Desert to Dakar, Senegal, on the west coast of Africa. Motorcycles and cars race in the event.

A touring motorcycle loaded with two riders, clothing, and camping gear

MOTORCYCLE
M I X

A two-stroke motorcycle engine does not have a separate oil lubrication system. Instead, oil is mixed with the gasoline to lubricate the cylinder and piston.

MOTORCYCLE
WHEELIES

Motorcycles built for drag racing have two small wheels on a bar behind the cycle. Known as a wheelie bar, it prevents the front wheel from rising off the ground as the motorcycle accelerates.

Farmers learned long ago of cycles' usefulness in crossing roadless land

MOTORCYCLES FOR RECREATION

Off-road motorcycles are built for travel over dirt roads or rugged trails. Compared to road motorcycles, they have light frames, better **suspension** to smooth the bumpy ride, and more room between the bottom of the engine and the ground so the engine does not hit large rocks or logs. Knobby tires give the bikes good traction in loose dirt, and the plastic fenders spring back after hitting obstacles such as boulders or trees. Many people ride off-road motorcycles for fun, but some farmers and ranchers rely on them to work in areas where roads have not been built. Rangers in national parks may ride motorcycles when their duties take them into the **backcountry**.

MOTORCYCLE
TIRES

In 1887, British inventor John Dunlop made air-inflated tires for use on tricycles. His tires were soon used on motorcycles since the cushion of air produced a more comfortable ride.

MOTORCYCLE
RECORD

The current land speed record for a motorcycle was set by a Harley-Davidson called the Easyrider Streamliner. In 1990, rider Dave Campos reached a speed of 322 miles (518 km) per hour.

Motocross is an exciting combination of speed and big jumps

M otorcycle racing is a popular sport for both riders and spectators. Motorcycles race on different kinds of tracks. Each type of racing requires specially built motorcycles and riders of exceptional ability. Motocross races are held on dirt tracks over rough **terrain** with steep hills and sharp curves. Motocross competitions are also held in large sports arenas. Temporary dirt tracks are built with twisty courses and steep hills that send motorcycles soaring into the air.

MOTORCYCLE

ISLAND

The famous Tourist Trophy motorcycle races were first held in 1911 on a 37.5-mile (60 km) course on the Isle of Man, an island between England and Ireland.

MOTORCYCLE

BEACH

Motorcycle races were held on the hard, white sand beach at Daytona Beach, Florida, from 1902 to 1959. The beach is 23 miles (37 km) long and 500 feet (152 m) wide at low tide.

Drag races are short races along a straight, paved track one-quarter of a mile (402 m) long. Two motorcycles compete side by side. The fastest drag racing motorcycles reach speeds of about 200 miles (322 km) per hour and reach the finish line in about six seconds.

MOTORCYCLE
STUNTS

American daredevil Evel Knievel became famous for his long motorcycle jumps. In 1975, he jumped a distance of 190 feet (58 m). During his career, he suffered many broken bones.

High-speed cycle racing involves only the most daring, skillful riders

MOTORCYCLE

After being out of business for almost 50 years, the Indian Motorcycle Company began making motorcycles again in 1999. The new Indians cost between $16,500 and $24,000.

28

MOTORCYCLE IMPROVEMENTS

Motorcycle makers are always competing with one another to attract customers. One way modern manufacturers have increased the **performance** and appeal of motorcycles is by making them lighter. Instead of steel, they use aluminum and other lightweight metal **alloys** for frames and engines. Strong but light plastic and carbon fiber materials are often used instead of metal in making fenders.

Some motorcycle riders carry their spare gear in leather pouches that hang over the rear wheel. The leather pouches, called saddlebags, are like those used by cowboys.

Manufacturers strive to improve rider comfort as well. A motorcyclist must be able to comfortably reach all of the controls with his or her hands and feet. In the future, small electric motors will automatically adjust the height of the seat, length of the handlebars, and placement of the pedals to the size of the rider.

A motorcycle built 30 years ago (left), and a lighter one of today (far left)

MOTORCYCLE
PARTY

*Each year in August, thousands of motorcycle riders gather for a week-long **rally** in the small town of Sturgis, South Dakota.*

Many people believe the open road is best traveled on two wheels

Today, motorcycles are designed to meet the different needs of different riders. Lightweight and fuel-efficient motorcycles are built for riders looking for an inexpensive way to get around. Big, powerful motorcycles with large fuel tanks are designed for riders who enjoy the freedom of gliding along the open highway. But no matter what a motorcycle's size or shape, these two-wheeled machines are a fun way to travel.

Glossary

Alloys are mixtures (usually strong and lightweight) of two or more metals.

The **backcountry** is a wilderness area without roads or other services.

The **clutch** is a lever that briefly separates a motorcycle's engine from its chain so the rider can change gears.

A **crankshaft** is an engine part that turns the up-and-down motion of a piston into a rotating motion.

An **enduro** race is a long motorcycle race in harsh conditions; enduro is a shortened form of the word "endurance."

Gas mileage is a measure of the amount of fuel a vehicle uses relative to the distance traveled.

Medics are emergency medical personnel who ride in ambulances and treat sick or injured people.

Performance is the overall rating of a motorcycle, including its gas mileage, acceleration, and handling.

A **rally** is a gathering of people with a common interest, such as owners of the same brand of motorcycle.

Sidecars are one-wheeled carts built onto the side of motorcycles; a sidecar has a seat for a passenger.

A **spark plug** is a part that generates electric sparks to ignite the gas and air mixture in an engine.

The **suspension** is the collection of springs between the wheels and frame of a motorcycle; it produces a smoother ride.

Terrain is the surface of the earth; off-road motorcycles are used on rugged terrain.

The **throttle** is a valve that gives a motorcycle engine more or less gasoline and thus changes the bike's speed.

Index